POCKET IMAGES

Newtown

Newtown Football Club's most memorable year. Frank Francis and Bobby Hibbott with the Montgomeryshire Cup, one of three they won in 1955 (see p. 121).

POCKET IMAGES

Newtown

Newtown Local History Group

Trefor Davies, Miles James, Brian Jones, Elwyn
Jones, June McColley, Mary Oldham, Nixon Oliver,
David Pugh, Allan Roberts, Margaret Stacey, Les
Stott and John Syers

Introduction and captions written by
David Pugh

NONSUCH

The Old Church in about 1900.

First published 1995
This new pocket edition 2006
Images unchanged from first edition

Nonsuch Publishing Limited
The Mill, Brimscombe Port,
Stroud, Gloucestershire, GL5 2QG
www.nonsuch-publishing.com

Nonsuch Publishing is an imprint of Tempus Publishing Group

British Library Cataloguing in Publication Data.
A catalogue record for this book is available from the British Library.

ISBN 1-84588-300-4

Typesetting and origination by Nonsuch Publishing Limited
Printed in Great Britain by Oaklands Book Services Limited

Contents

Acknowledgements

We would like to thank all those who lent us photographs for inclusion in this book, amongst whom were:

Andy Antoniazzi, Frank Bennett-Lloyd, Edmund Davies, the Misses Hamer, Cliff Hamer, Terrill Hawkins, Joan Hughes, Bert Jones, Heulwen Jones, Joe Jones, June Jones, Kath Jones, Tony Leach, Barbara Lewis, Freda Lewis, Fred Lovell, Marjorie Meredith, Alan Morgan, Newtown and Llanllwchaiarn Town Council, Andrew Owen, Cliff Owen, John Passant, John Poulton, Michael Poulton, Megan Powell, Malcolm Pryce, Mrs H. Snead, Joan Stephenson, Pam Stott, Nita Taylor, Les Wilkins, Alan Williams, Joy Williams.

We would also like to thank the photographers, many of them anonymous, who took the trouble to record the passing scene in Newtown.

Finally, cheers to Mrs Kath Thomas who allowed us to occupy a warm corner of the bar in The Bell Hotel whilst putting this book together.

Introduction

Newtown formally came into existence as a market town when in 1279 it was granted a charter by Edward I. For the next five hundred years it remained a small economic centre for the surrounding agricultural area. Then, at the end of the eighteenth century it began a period of change than was to see it expand from a sleepy market town with a population of less than a thousand to a busy industrial centre sustaining nearly ten times that number. The raw material of this revolution was wool. The hills of Montgomeryshire supported thousands of sheep and the rain which fell on those hills ran into the brooks and streams feeding the River Severn to form a powerful source of energy. Weirs were thrown across the river and the flow used to drive the huge waterwheels of the mills built on the banks. Welsh flannel from Newtown became known across the world.

By the time of the period covered by this book the woollen industry had begun its terminal decline. The development of steam power had overtaken that of water. Newtown could not compete with Yorkshire which had coal, and large markets, on its doorstep. People began to leave the town. Some took their specialist skills to Yorkshire, others went to the South Wales coalfield. Yet more emigrated to America, Australia or South Africa to pursue often colourful careers.

Throughout the first half of the twentieth century the population of the town steadily declined. By the 1960s it had become clear that, unless there was government intervention, Mid-Wales would become almost entirely depopulated. Intervention came in the form of the Mid-Wales Development Corporation, later reformed as the Development Board for Rural Wales, which was set up to reverse this trend. In the last thirty years new houses have been built, new industries introduced, and the face of the town transformed. The population is now over ten thousand, greater than it ever was when Newtown was 'The Busy Leeds of Wales'.

It is beyond the scope of this book to chronicle in great detail these changes. What it can aspire to do, however, is to provide a series of snap-shots, literally, of the changing face of our town and the lives of the people in it. Anyone wishing to get a more coherent view of the historical background of the town could do no better that read the late Maurice Richards' *A History of Newtown*, published by the Powysland Club in 1993.

Newtown Local History Group is an informal gathering of people who are interested in collecting and conserving material relating to Newtown's past. We are very grateful to those people who have lent us photographs, often of great personal value, for inclusion in this book. What has become clear during the preparation of the book is that there is still a lot of material in existence that we have not been able to find, and worse, there was material of important historical interest that has been inadvertently destroyed. We would be pleased to hear from anyone who is prepared to pass to us, or lend for copying, written or pictorial material, or indeed join us in putting together the pieces of the many strands of our local history.

We have done our best to check the accuracy of the information in this book but doubtless there remain errors within it. We would again like to hear from anyone who can correct or add to what appears in these pages. We can be contacted c/o Rhoswen, Bryn Street, Newtown, Powys, SY16 2HW.

One

People

Mochdre Mill, c. 1900.

A dynasty of woollen manufacturers. John Leach (seated, wearing bowler hat) came to Mochdre Mill from Pool Quay with his father, James Leach, about 1848. When James died in 1872, John took over the business and ran it until his own death in 1916, when his son, also John Henry (third left, back row) took control. John Henry decided to retire after the mill had been badly damaged by the flood of June 1936 and passed the business to his son, Seymour Stanhope Leach (the small boy holding the donkey on the right). When he took over, Seymour advertised that he made farmers' own wool into blankets, car rugs, bed rugs, tweeds and Welsh yarn. He was a man of great mechanical ingenuity, managing to keep the antiquated machinery in the mill, much of it dating back to the mid-nineteenth century, in production until his death in 1962. The mill and its machinery were then sold, bringing woollen manufacture in the Newtown area to an end.

Above: Much has been written (and many illustratrations made) about the woollen industry in the town. Many of the old buildings remained in residential or other use until removed by the Development Board in the 1970s. This is the old Club Factory in New Church Street as it looked shortly before it was demolished. The upper storeys of the factory had been removed some years earlier.

Right: A family group outside their house in the Club Factory before it was altered. It was common for the walls of buildings, particularly the west walls, to be slated against the driving Welsh rain. The location of the house in the factory is clearly identifiable from the large porch over the door.

The picture of the family on their doorstep on the previous page comes from a collection of glass plate negatives found in a fireplace of an old house on The Bank in 1963. Nothing is known of their origin but they all seem to have been taken about the 1920s. There was no information with them to say who the people were, or where they were taken. Some are clearly identifiable and appear in later sections of this book. Others require a little more detective work, like the one above. It is of the Old Toll House in Commercial Street. The house has changed greatly since the photograph was taken, but the arrangement of the stones in the wall in the bottom right of the picture remains the same to this day. It might seem odd that a toll house should be set back from the road and sideways on to it, but before the Penygloddfa area was developed for the expanding woollen industry in the 1820s and 1830s, Frankwell Street was the main road out of the town. It continued across what is now Commercial Street right past the front door of the Old Toll House and joined the present Llanfair Road near the junction with Bryn Lane. The anonymous photographer specialised in pictures of people on their doorsteps and some of them are reproduced on the following pages. The compilers of this book would be pleased to hear from anyone who could provide more information about this remarkable collection of pictures.

The sisters Nellie, Ginnie and Lizzie Morgan on their doorstep in Sheaf Street, 1920s. The street has long gone but the oak tree in the background remains as part of the Treowen estate.

An unidentified couple on their doorstep at No 4 Lower Canal Road, 1920s.

Sheaf Street, 1920s showing Bessie Roberts, with her daughter Patty.

Family group, probably pictured outside the Club Factory, 1920s.

14

Two

The Royal Welsh
Warehouse Sports

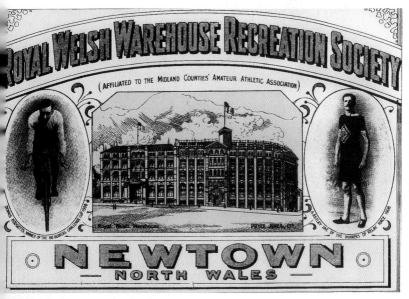

Part of the poster for the Royal Welsh Warehouse (RWW) Sports and Musical Festival held on 12 June 1909.

Above: An early programme for the sports, with a reminder that the RWW Recreation Association also arranged rail excursions to popular resorts.

Left: A major feature of the sports were cycle races with professional riders from all over Britain attracted by the large cash prizes offered. The RWW had its own cycling club, whose riders were doubtless prepared to take on all-comers.

RULES.

1.—That this Club be called the "R. W. W. Cycling Club," and that it be strictly confined to members of the Recreation and Improvement Society.

2.—That the affairs of the Club be managed by a Committee to consist of the Officers, and not more than five other members (five to form a quorum), who shall all be elected at a General Meeting called "Yearly" for that purpose.

3.—That the Club runs take place as arranged by the Committee—members to meet opposite Clifton Terrace (unless otherwise stated).

4.—That the Captain shall have full command at all meetings for exercises, tours, &c., or in his absence the Deputy Captain.

5.—That in all Club runs the helmet with badge selected must be worn; but no member shall wear the Club badge *on Sundays*.

6.—That any member may be allowed to introduce a friend to the meets or ordinary runs.

7.—That the Committee shall have full power to call Special Meetings of the Club for any purpose, to expel any member upon due cause being shown (subject to the approval of a General Meeting), to suspend any Officer, to inflict fines for disobedience, and do all such other acts as they may deem necessary for carrying out the objects of the Club.

8.—That the Badges and Bugles be the property of the Club, and that all members must return same (or any property they may have belonging to the Club) at end of Season (or when leaving) to the Secretary.

9.—That a copy of these Rules be supplied to every member who shall be bound by same.

10.—That these Rules be subject to alteration by a General Meeting.

RULES OF THE ROAD.

1.—That in all runs and tours the Captain shall lead, (or in his absence the Deputy Captain), and any member wilfully over-running him without his permission, shall be fined 6d. for each offence.

2.—That the Deputy Captain shall bring up the rear, and look after stragglers (if any), and when necessary call a halt, or slower pace.

3.—That all orders shall be given by bugle call; those by the Captain to be repeated by the Deputy Captain, and *vice versa*.

4.—THAT THE FOLLOWING BE THE BUGLE CALLS—
Mount..........Three short notes.
Dismount........Two   ,,
Slower..........One prolonged ,,
Quicker........Succession of ,,

5.—That on meeting any horse or conveyance, members shall go on the left hand side, and on overtaking any vehicle, shall do so on the right hand side; but on meeting or passing a horse, take that side of the road on which the man is who is leading the animal.

6.—That all members must carry bell, wrench, oil can, and when riding after dark a lighted lamp.

7.—That no smoking be allowed while passing through towns or villages, and that path riding be prohibited.

NOTE.—*It is particularly requested that these Rules be strictly observed, and that uniform politeness be shewn by members to everyone, so that an untarnished reputation may be gained.*

To celebrate the granting of a knighthood to Sir Pryce Pryce-Jones in 1887 the staff of his Royal Welsh Warehouse held a sports day. Members of the Pryce-Jones family were keen sportsmen and subsequently they formed a recreation society for their employees. The sports became an annual event and each year more attractions were added and the event drew bigger crowds. Musical competitions were introduced, including brass band contests, choral and solo competitions. The main events were held on the Royal Welsh Warehouse's own sports ground on Pool Road (now the Recreation Ground). There was also a brass band quick step competition. This took place in Broad Street and the Cross, the bands marching from the Public Rooms (now the Regent Centre) to The Lion Hotel. The adjudicator was placed either on the balcony of The Bear Hotel or in a window above one of the shops in the Cross Buildings. Adjudicators frequently complained that they could not hear the bands for the cheering of the crowds.

Soon after the 1914 sports the First World War broke out. When peace finally came there was an attempt to revive the event but attendances were poor. Before the war special trains had brought thousands of people, many of them old Newtonians, from the coalfields of South Wales, but by 1919 the miners were in bitter dispute with the coal owners. Neither they nor their families could afford to renew the old tradition.

Above: the RWW Cycling Club rules. They were clearly a highly disciplined group, riding to the instructions sounded by their bugler. Note also their rules concerning the wearing of club badges on Sundays and smoking whilst passing through towns or villages.

PROGRAMME OF EVENTS.

Bicycle Races under N.C.U. rules. Permit granted by Liverpool Centre N.C.U.

Handicapper: Mr. H. P. ELLIS, LIVERPOOL. N.B.---All Cyclists must have licences.

	FIRST PRIZE.	SECOND PRIZE.	ENTRANCE FEE.
Two Mile Bicycle Handicap (open)	Marble Clock. Value £3 : 3 : 0. *Presented by Col. Pryce-Jones, M.P.*	H.M. Silver Double Albert. Value £1 : 1 : 0.	1/- each event or
One Mile Bicycle Handicap (open)	H.M. Gold Medal. Value £2 : 10 : 0.	Electro-Plated Cruet. Value £1 : 1 : 0.	1/6 for both.
Tug of War, six a side, (open) (No Spikes allowed).	£1 : 5 : 0 (cash).	10/6 (cash).	1/6 per team.

The following events are confined to the Employes of PRYCE JONES, Ltd.

440 yards Flat Handicap.	H.M. Silver Cigarette Case.	H.M. Silver Albert.	3d.
Obstacle Race (one lap).	Time Piece. *Presented by A. W. Pryce-Jones, Esq.*	H.M. Gold Scarf Pin.	3d.
120 yards Boys' Handicap. For Boys under 18 years.	H.M. Gold-Centre Medal. *Presented by W. E. Pryce-Jones, Esq.*	H.M. Silver Medal.	3d.
Sack Race.	Pair of Bronze Ornaments.	Silver-mounted Walking Stick.	3d.
220 yards Flat Handicap.	Set of Carvers.	Crumb Brush and Tray.	3d.
High Jump.	Gent's Umbrella.	Cigarette Holder.	3d.
Throwing the Cricket Ball.	Butter Dish.	H.M. Silver Scarf Pin.	3d.
Tug of War (six a side) (No Spikes allowed)	£1 : 0 : 0 (cash). *Presented by Sir Pryce Pryce-Jones.*	10/- (cash).	1/6 per team.
Bowls (partners drawn)	Two H.M. Silver Match Boxes.	Two Briar Pipes.	3d.
Quoits (partners drawn)	Two Briar Pipes.	Two Pocket Knives.	3d.
Tennis (partners drawn)	Two Electro-Plated Biscuit Boxes *Presented by Lady Pryce-Jones.*	Two Silver Pencil Cases.	3d.

Entries close as follows:

For the Three Open Events, viz :—Bicycle Races and Tug of War, Saturday, June 17th, (Monday Morning's Post in time).

For the Events confined to Employes of PRYCE JONES, LTD., Wednesday, June 14th.

SEE BACK PAGE.]

Secretary: Evan Humphreys, Royal Welsh Warehouse, Newtown.

The programme of events for the sports of 22 June 1899. Note the value of the prizes. At that time £1 would have bought more than 200 pints of beer.

The tug-of-war at the 1906 sports. The competitors were not allowed to wear spiked shoes.

A competitor passes the makeshift grandstand. The tarpaulin roof to the stand was borrowed from the Cambrian Railways. Note the pendulum clock on the centre post.

Another version of the grandstand from a different year. This photograph is credited to Osborne Edwards, one of two brothers who ran a photographic business in High Street until after the Second World War.

Modern technology was employed to ensure the smooth running of the 1906 sports. One of the joint secretaries, F.P. Keay, who was also company secretary of the RWW, uses the field telephone watched by his fellow secretary, Evan Humphreys. Fred Keay was also active in amateur dramatic and musical performances in the town. It was considered to be a great loss to the town when he emigrated to Chicago in 1909 to join a family business.

A group of officials discuss matters between events. Evan Humphreys is in the centre with his hands beneath the back of his jacket.

The final of the 1906 tug-of-war – Manchester Police vs Liverpool Police. They were to meet again in the final the following year. The Mancunians were victorious on both occasions.

The hurdle race in 1906. Failure to clear the substantial fixed hurdle must have exacted a heavy penalty. The photograph was taken in the south-eastern corner of the field. The railway line can be seen in the background.

Action sports photography with small compact cameras using fast film was a long way in the future in 1906. The photographers of cycle races at that time overcame considerable difficulties to get these shots.

Four competitors complete another lap. The Rock Farm can be seen in the background.

The start of the three mile scratch race in 1906. The white lines across the track marked the different starting positions for handicap races.

The winners of the final of the one mile race cross the decorated finishing line in 1906.

In its heyday the RWW sports drew crowds of up to 20,000 people.

The band contest drew top names from all over the country. It would appear that the contestants played standing up and only drew passing interest from the crowd.

Right: H. Minton, winner of the three-mile scratch race in 1906.

Below: An exciting finish to the final heat of the three mile 60 guinea challenge cup competition in June 1905.

No wonder the adjudicators had difficulty in hearing the competitors. A band gets virtually lost among the thousands thronging Broad Street during the quickstep contest.

A novel feature of the 1913 sports was the first ever flying display in Newtown by the renowned Gustav Hamil. He made three flights. For many it was the first time they had seen powered flight. The *Montgomeryshire Express* declared that it was 'a magnificent and memorable performance.' Afterwards Hamil's machine was displayed, dismantled and placed on the back of a lorry, outside Jones Bros. Garage (now Newtown Motor Garage) on Pool Road.

The following year, Hamil was booked to fly again but a month before the sports he was reported 'missing presumed killed' on a flight across the English Channel. Hamil's place was taken by Frank Gooden, seen here with his Morane Saulnier in which he gave 'a thrilling and sensational exhibition of aeroplane flights including looping the loop and upside down flying.' In February 1917 the *Express* reported that Gooden too had been killed. His plane had broken up whilst flying at 2,000 feet.

Three

Events

For King George V's Silver Jubilee year in 1935 the carnival queen became the jubilee queen. This picture is from the back of a small hand mirror (about 5 cm across) made to commemorate the event.

Newtown has a tradition of annual carnivals dating back to the 1890s, but the carnival in its present form was started in 1929 by Llanllwchaiarn Women's Institute as a means of raising funds for the County Infirmary. The event always started with a procession through the town starting, in the early years, in the Back Lane. Mrs Fanny Edwards poses, above, with her float of young ladies outside Morris's builders' yards (where the entrance to the bus station and car park is now).

The procession ended in the grounds of Newtown Hall, then the residence of the Arbuthnot-Brisco family, where the queen was crowned. Here the 1951 queen, Gwyneth Owen, poses with her entourage having just been crowned by Mrs Senator Rupert Davies who is seated, wearing a hat, on the extreme left.

The girls of the Congregational Chapel depict *Swan Lake* for the 1957 carnival.

In 1934, Miss Montgomeryshire, Freda Garnett took the place of honour on the Pryce-Jones float.

Left: Local butcher and well-known singer, Watkin Dodd poses in the costume he devised for the 1930 carnival.

Below: In the 1950s 'Queen' Jessie Blayney prepares to set out from the old grammar school with her entourage.

A feature of the carnival for many years was the dance troupes, then sometimes called morris-dancers, although they bore little relation to what we now understand by the term. The first of these became known as 'The Pony Dancers'. Trained by Phyllis and Winnie Bailey they first appeared under that name in 1933 and here they pose for the camera in the Crescent during the carnival of that year.

The Pony Dancers did not reappear in 1934, but the following year a group which contained many former members appeared at local shows and carnivals performing what they called 'The Dinkie Blue Cabaret'. This photograph was taken that year.

DINKIE BLUES 1936

By 1936 the group had grown in number and was then called The Dinkie Blues. Under this name they continued to delight carnival crowds well into the 1950s. In this traditional 'chorus girl' line up photographed in 1936, from left to right: Ruth Boulton, Phyllis Jones, Winnie Crewe, Peggy Ridgewell, Constance Doyle, Marjorie Lumsden, Dorothy Brandrick, Mary Barrett, Gwyneth Williams, Jenny Lesser, Joy Challinor, Mair Jones, Irene Dodd, Thelma Lloyd, Patty Jones, Winnie Bailey, Gwyneth Owen, Eileen Matthews, Florence Hibbott, and in front their mascot, Hilda Davies.

It was not only carnivals that brought people out onto the streets to watch processions. The Jubilee of King George V and Queen Mary on 6 May 1935 was celebrated in the usual way. Here Newtown Silver Band, followed by the members of the Urban District Council lead the procession pass The Bear Hotel.

A few minutes later the children of the town pass the same point. After the procession they were treated to tea and sports and were presented with mugs.

The people of the Ladywell area had a reputation for lavishly decorating their streets. As they had little money to spare, a great deal of improvisation was necessary. The decoration of Ladywell Street for the 1935 Jubilee, seen here from the eastern end, so impressed the rest of the town that there was a proposal that the street should be renamed 'Jubilee Street'.

Just around the corner in Frolic Street, the residents pose for the photographer amidst their decorations. The man in the flat cap on the extreme left is Ivo Smith, who was at that time the proprietor of The Bear Hotel.

The pictures across the top of these two pages were found as separate prints but clearly come from the same negative. They show the inhabitants of Ladywell out in the street to celebrate the Coronation of George VI in 1937. Perhaps old Newtonians would like to see how many well-known faces they can identify in the crowd!

Coronation celebrations in Ladywell, 1937.

Sixteen years later Ladywell was again decorated as lavishly as ever. But by 1953 television had arrived in the town and the streets were empty.

New Church in 1953, just as profusely decorated, and just as deserted. Note the Club Factory on the right (see p. 11).

The shops were shut on Coronation Day 1953, but nevertheless the shopkeepers decorated them. This is Bert Evans' shop in Short Bridge Street. Although John Roberts had died in 1937, the year of the previous coronation, his name remained over the shop.

The manager of the Gas Shop, Harold Evans OBE ('Harold the Gas') also made sure that his showroom was suitably adorned for the occasion.

A few hardy souls braved the bitterly cold June weather for the aquatic sports held on the river for Coronation Day, 1953. Here local businessmen Ken Dodd and Richie Richards are piloted past a lone competitor in the raft race.

Four

Redevelopment

Whitney's Shop in Park Street in 1968.

All towns change as social and economic pressures lead to the alteration and replacement of buildings to meet changing needs. What was unusual about Newtown was the rate of change that took place in the 1960s and 1970s. These changes were brought about by two agencies. Firstly there were the catastrophic floods that took place in 1960 and 1964, which are dealt with in more detail in section seven. The second, and more far-reaching, engine of change was the creation of the Mid Wales Development Corporation in 1967. A committee that had reported to the government in 1964 found that rural depopulation would continue unabated unless urgent measures were taken to stop it. The outcome was the setting up of the Development Corporation with the task of bringing new industries to the area and at least doubling the size of Newtown. To achieve this, large areas of the town had to be demolished and rebuilt in a different form. The above picture shows what was left in 1971 of Ladywell Street and New Church Street, seen decorated in the previous section. The decorations have gone, the houses have gone and most importantly, the people have gone. The town had changed for ever. Ladywell House and St David's House now occupy this site.

Lower Ladywell Street looking east towards Short Bridge Street before demolition had been completed. The building on the right with the tarpaulin on the roof was part of the complex of buildings that formed Samuel Powell's Ladywell Brewery. It had recently been badly damaged by fire. The white building on the left was up until 1936 The Elms Inn. It was latterly the home of Mr Bernie Pryce and family.

The yard behind The Elms. Bernie Pryce would buy and sell most things, but not the goose that stood in the window. Many offers were made, but none accepted. The goose, being made of papier maché, finally disintegrated.

Left: The Brewery buildings flank the oddly named Butterfly Lane which led from Lower Ladywell Street to New Road. The lane was at one time known as Ladywell Court.

Below: Almost opposite the end of Butterfly Lane and just along from The Elms, part of which is visible on the right, stood Crown Mill House. The garage on the right-hand end of the building once housed the town's fire engine.

Victor Davies ('Lamp Oil') and Mrs Liz Evans look remarkably cheerful as they stand in front of what was No 21 Ladywell Street, on the corner with New Church Street.

New Church Street photographed from the present-day traffic lights on New Road. The Board School (the name was officially changed to Newtown Council School in 1902, but the old name stuck) is on the left. The junior school was housed in the classrooms that ran along by New Road on the left and the infants were in the rooms beyond the main entrance. On the right is the (modified) Club Factory referred to in section one. The only buildings that remain are the Congregational Church and Schoolroom beyond the school.

The Congregational Schoolroom locates these four houses, Nos 52 to 55, Upper Ladywell Street. Behind all the houses facing on to the streets in this area there were more houses squeezed into courts and places. The passageway between Nos 53 and 54 led to Bostock Place (see p. 128).

The clearance of the south side of Upper Ladywell Street gave a clear view of the north side, running from Frolic Street on the left to the houses seen on the previous page to the right.

A closer view of the end of Upper Ladywell Street. At Frolic Street are the houses fronting Compton Place; the gate between the railings was the rear entrance to the Victoria Hall and the passageway between the houses on the right led to Jones Court.

Looking across what was once the south side of Upper Ladywell to the backs of buildings on New Road and Frolic Street. On the left is the Domestic Subjects Centre built by the Education Authority in 1911 and on the right the building and lorry body that were part of the haulage business run by Mr T.E. Woodhouse.

The north end of Frolic Street looking towards Park Street, and Newtown Hall Grounds (The Park) beyond. The buildings were demolished, like most of the others in the preceding few pages, c. 1971.

Above: Park Street, which lay to the north of Ladywell, remains but many of its older buildings have gone. The church in this picture was built as the second Wesleyan Methodist church in 1821. By 1833 it had proved to be too small, so in 1835 the Methodists moved to their new church in Severn Place. Next to the church, on the right, stood The Picton Arms Inn and the stone-fronted shop beyond was for many years occupied by Morgan Davies, tailor.

Right: At the rear of The Picton Arms stood Picton's Row. It was typical of the back-to-back developments that were thrown up to accommodate the rapidly developing woollen industry in the first half of the nineteenth century. Around the other side, to the left, was an identical row of cottages, and over them all was the shared workroom containing the looms.

Next to Morgan Davies' shop stood this building, seen here near the end of its varied life. It was built in 1803 as a Baptist chapel, enlarged in 1814 and again in 1821 reflecting the success of the denomination. In 1881 the Baptists moved to their present site on New Road. The old building was sold and turned into the town's second theatre, the first being the Public Hall. It was named the Victoria Hall and staged a wide range of professional and amateur musical and dramatic entertainments. It was also used for the annual Newtown Eisteddfod on New Year's Day and for public meetings; Lloyd-George spoke there twice. In 1910 it was taken over by a showman named John Codman, who converted it into 'The Picturedrome' – the town's first cinema. In 1917 it was taken over by W. Truman Dicken, who tried to re-introduce live entertainment along with the films. 'What ever is best in Pictures, in Variety, in Plays or in other Clean and Healthy Entertainment', he advertised. It was not a success. The following year he converted the building back into a cinema. At that time films were still silent so the music was provided by the famous Hunter Bell Family Orchestra who lived further up Park Street. During the Second World War it was requisitioned as a military store and used as the Naafi. Afterwards it remained a warehouse. Its final user was Mr Charlie Evans who later took over the old Co-op in Market Street as 'Charlie's Store'.

The rear of the Victoria Hall while it was under demolition in 1972. The brickwork shows evidence of its varied life.

A continuation of the south side of Park Street with Morgan Davies' shop on the left. The shop on the corner of Frolic Street – No 17 Park Street – was, in the early years of the century, Humphreys grocer's shop and later, up to the time of its demolition, Whitney's gun and bicycle shop.

Another Park Street building that is no longer with us. It was the County Library, built to replace the earlier County Library in Severn Place. It did not fall to re-development but to a disastrous fire in April 1986. Although much of the contents were destroyed, Newtown Fire Brigade were able to save the priceless local history collection, from which much of the historical information in this book has been gathered.

One of the oldest buildings in Park Street is No 47, which remains little changed to this day. It was originally the farmhouse of a dairy farm. The cows were kept on the fields now occupied by Hafren and Ladywell Green schools. This picture was taken in the 1920s.

Right: Another part of old Newtown which disappeared in the 1970s was the Skinner Street/Weir Street area. This view is of Skinner Street from the corner of Severn Square; No 8 is on the left. On the right is Lewis & Sons Tannery.

Below: Skinner Street from the Old Church Street end. The other end of the 'tunnel' through the building can be seen. Before the tannery was relocated to the Pool Road, it occupied most of the area where St Mary's Close now stands.

Left: The tannery buildings extended to Crown Street. The sign over the entrance says 'Lewis & Son, Entrance for Hides.' Most of the buildings in the distance remain, including those in Severn Street.

Below: The rear of the buildings in Severn Square and the tannery from the river bank. The end of the old Halfpenny Bridge can be seen on the right.

Severn Square remains much the same except that the tannery, with its distinctive chimney has gone. The house on the left was demolished to make way for the new access road to St Mary's Close and Old Church Street. It was once the home of B. Bennett-Rowlands who published a history of Newtown in 1914. The double-fronted house next to it was for some years the home of Mr Hugh Lewis, the proprietor of the tannery.

Severn Place still exists, but it is now considered to be part of Back Lane. The name has gone, and so have many of the buildings in this picture of about 1968, taken from the west end looking towards Broad Street and The Elephant and Castle.

Above: 'Around the corner' in Severn Place. The picture on the previous page was taken from behind the car on the left. The building on the left remains as the Territorial Army HQ. Like many of the large old buildings in the town it started life as a wool warehouse, and was at one time occupied by a Mr Blyth. The slated building on the right was also a wool warehouse, Morgan and Morgan's and then Jones Bros.

Left: The Army has been in Blyth's Warehouse for many years. This inscription on the east wall at one time said: 'The Headquarters, 7th Vol. Battalion, The Royal Welch Fusiliers'. Those words have now almost completely weathered off and in this 1994 photograph an earlier wording can be seen. It says 'The Head Quarters, 5th Vol Battalion, South Wales Borderers'. The 5th SWB, who had served in the Boer War, were disbanded in 1908 and replaced in that year by the 7th RWF.

Right: In 1935 Jones' Wool Warehouse, which had stood empty for many years, was bought by the Montgomeryshire Community Recreation Association who spent over £2,000 converting it for community use. It became the home of the YMCA, the MCRA itself, the Ministry of Labour and the county's WIs. Other rooms were made available for hire by other community organisations. The building was, logically, given the name Community House.

Below: This picture looks across what used to be 'The Cunnings,' a piece of ground used for football matches, open air concerts and other public activities. Community House is just left of centre and on the right the original single storey clubhouse of Newtown Bowling Club. Behind it stands the massive bulk of the Wesleyan Methodist Church.

This was the third Wesleyan chapel in the town, built to replace the one on Park Street (see p. 51). After it was demolished it was replaced, on the same site, by the present building.

The present chapel, pictured in 1987, before the south wing was added.

Five

The Town Centre

A drawing of 'The Checkers' by Reginald M. Copnall which won a prize at the 1896 Newtown Eisteddfod.

Although Newtown's centre has not been dramatically changed by the development of the town, alterations have taken place over the years, not always without controversy. There was much opposition to the demolition of the old Checkers Inn ('Hotel de Straw Hat') which was said to be the last thatched building in any town in Montgomeryshire. The little shop on the right was at various times a grocer's, a fish and chip shop and a saddler's. This picture was taken before 1905 as Mr Smout, the landlord, died in that year.

In 1931 The Checkers lost its licence 'due to redundancy' and it was subsequently bought by Mr J. Cookson, already proprietor of three garages in the town, who intended to build a car showroom on the site. In the event Peacock's Stores, who were looking for a site in the town, made him a good offer and he sold it to them. Peacock's opened their store in 1934. It was taken over as an Admiralty store in 1939 and remained empty for some years after the war. The shop is now occupied by the Spar supermarket.

Broad Street in the 1930s, shortly after Peacock's Store opened.

A little way up Broad Street from The Checkers stood The Black Boy Hotel. It remains there, but has now lost its railings. The shop to the right is Clayton's China and Fancy Goods, and the door next to it is the entrance to Powell's, later Powell & Ridout, Bournemouth House. This business was moved across the road to No 19 Broad Street in 1912. These shops were badly damaged in the 1960s flood and subsequently replaced with Pearl Assurance House.

This picture, taken in the 1880s, links those on the previous two pages. At that time the buildings next to The Black Boy were private houses. Next to The Checkers is Croft's Shoes. This was a shoe shop until 1993.

BROAD STREET, NEWTOWN.   204322 JV

The south end of Broad Street in the 1930s. On the right can be seen part of the National Provincial Bank, replaced in the 1970s by the NatWest. Next to it is Phillips' Music Salon which sold all manner of musical instruments, sheet music, and 78 rpm gramophone records. No 1 High Street (then the offices of William Watkins, solicitor) to the right of the Town Clock still had its original roof at this time.

Broad Street from outside The Elephant & Castle, *c.* 1900. The first shop beyond the private houses on the right is Phillips' stationery shop, owned by W.P. Phillips, who was also the proprietor of the music salon. The building on the site of the present Woolworth's is The Blue Bell Inn, demolished in 1935 to make way for the new store.

View from The Cross in the early 1900s. The ornate shop-front next to the Free Library on the right is that of the Royal Bazaar, a drapers. Next to that is F.D. Clark's ironmonger's shop. Mr Clark was the father of the town's suffragette, Alix Minnie Clark. High up on the shop of Alfred Ford, jeweller, next door, can be seen the clock Mr Ford installed to celebrate Queen Victoria's Diamond Jubilee in 1897.

The Buck Inn was no doubt at one time thatched like The Checkers. It is now one of the oldest buildings remaining in the town. The land to the right of it was used as an auction yard before it became a garage in the 1920s.

High Street, seen here in the 1920s, has changed little except for the removal of the three buildings on the right to make way for Boots the Chemist, whose earlier premises can be seen with the sunblinds out further down the street.

This picture, the oldest in the book, was taken *c.* 1866. It shows the end of Short Bridge Street from the bottom of High Street. Although the location is still recognisable, none of the buildings in the picture remain. William Lewis' London House and The Oak Vaults next door were demolished in 1870 and rebuilt in 1872. The Oak Vaults lost its licence in 1903 as it had become 'the resort of loafers and loose women'. The shop on the right was demolished to make way for the present building in 1874. The curved building just visible on the left is part of Palmer's ironmonger's shop which was removed to make way for the Cross Buildings in 1899.

An early photograph of Short Bridge Street and the Bank. The stone wall on the right once formed the parapet to the Short Bridge built over the Green Brook in 1833. It was once renowned for its foul smells, a result of the primitive sanitary arrangements in the densely populated area upstream. The Green Brook was eventually culverted but 'The Bridge Wall' remains.

Above: Fred Lovell, left, and Terry McDermott at work with an oxy-acetylene cutter, one July morning, 1935. In 1920 a British tank and two captured German guns were placed on the land at the Bank. They had been given to the people of Newtown by the War Savings Commission 'to commemorate their notable subscriptions to War Securities during Guns Week 1918'. From the outset their presence was controversial. A number of attempts to have them removed were met with equally determined efforts to keep them there. Matters came to a head in 1935 when Cllr. David Lewis got 200 names on a petition to have them removed. On the evening of 1 July the Town Council asked their Clerk to obtain offers for the purchase and removal of the tank. The guns were to be removed to the Recreation Ground on Pool Road. The Town Clerk, solicitor Dickie George, must have moved quickly for by 7 o'clock the next morning men were at work cutting up the tank. The members of the British Legion were outraged. Highly charged public meetings were held, but the Town Council held firm. The guns stayed on 'the Rec' until they were removed for scrap during the Second World War and there was little that could be done about the tank. Its remains had already been loaded on to two railway wagons and despatched to Brymbo Steelworks, Wrexham.

Opposite below: The Bank in the 1890s from a slightly different angle, looking into Gas Street. The cobbled area to the left of the picture has an interesting history. Used in the nineteenth century as part of the horse market, it has never had a formal name, at one time it was just referred to as 'the land at the apex of The Bank'. In 1917 it became the home of the controversial 'War Trophies.'

After the trophies had been removed, the area was laid out as a park and encompassed by a wall and chains. The park was opened in July 1936 and dedicated to the memory of King George V, but never formally named after him.

The Robert Owen Museum Committee had asked for permission to place a statue of Robert Owen there before the park was opened, but in the event the unveiling did not take place until 21 April 1956. Arthur Jones, Secretary of the Appeals Committee (wearing glasses) stands by the newly unveiled statue.

The platform party at the unveiling. On the right sit Sir George and Lady Hamer, parents of the present Lady Hooson.

The Robert Owen Museum (seen here in its original location over the Midland Bank in Broad Street, on the site of Owen's birthplace) commemorates the life of Newtown's most famous son. Robert Owen (1771-1858) was a pioneer in social reform and his ideas led to the formation of the Co-operative Movement. Anyone wishing to know more of this remarkable man is urged to visit the present museum which is housed in the Free Library building opposite the Midland Bank.

The statue of Robert Owen, designed by Gilbert Bayes and constructed at a cost of £2,600. In 1994 it was removed for a few months to be cleaned and copied. In May of that year the copy was unveiled outside the headquarters of the Co-operative Bank in Balloon Street, Manchester.

Six

Shops

High Street, *c.* 1960. Traders secured the right to sell their wares in the streets of Newtown each Tuesday on 16 January 1279 and have been coming to the town on Tuesdays ever since.

Above: Clement W. Norton opened his ironmonger's shop in Broad Street *c.* 1882. In 1901 he was obliged to move to No 14 Broad Street as the owner of the property, Mrs Frances Arbuthnot, having inherited it from her aunt, Miss Sarah Brisco, wanted to carry out her aunt's instructions and donate the site of the shop and The Kings Head next door for the erection of a free library.

Left: C.W. Norton remained at No 14 Broad Street until 1913 when he handed over the business to Lloyd & Lloyd, seen here in the 1920s. He then ran a garage business in premises in Severn Street behind his old shop. He finally retired in 1919.

Clement Norton with his two sons. Both boys served in the First World War. Edgar, on the left became a lieutenant in the Army and died of malaria in Palestine in 1918. Ernest, right, was the first man in Montgomeryshire to learn to fly. He flew with the Royal Naval Air Service and was awarded the DSC. After the war he continued his career in the RAF, rising to the rank of Air Commodore.

Left: A few doors up from Norton's original shop, in what had been Alfred Ford's jewellers. The Jones family opened their sweetshop, The Bon-Bon, in 1918. The business was moved to No 27 Broad Street in 1930 and three years later, on the death of Mr Llewellyn Jones, was subsumed into Mr Evan Evans' confectionery business. Here Madge Jones stands outside No 50 Broad Street, now a salad and sandwich bar.

Below: Bunford's Store, Broad Street, *c.* 1920. The sign above claims that the business had already been established for over a hundred years. About 1946 it was taken over by Phillips Stores of Shrewsbury and is now Thrifty, outfitters. The two young men in aprons are thought to be the Lloyd brothers of Milford.

Below: A rare interior shot of a shop. The staff of Peacocks (see p. 62) line up behind their counters in the late 1930s.

Right: Croft's shoe shop (see p. 64) in the 1920s. Note the sign for the 'Express Offices.' The *Montgomeryshire Express* was printed and published in Old Church Street.

Left: W.S. Thompson took over the plumbing business at No 17 Broad Street from Philip Pritchard in 1921. By 1928 it had become Richards' sweet shop and is now a shoe repairers.

Below: The Elephant Hotel, as it was then styled, before the balcony was added. The sign to the left of the entrance has been recently altered to show Tuesday opening hours of 11 a.m. to 10 p.m., suggesting that this photograph was taken in 1928, the year this change took place.

Right: Pugh's Hotel and Cafe in Market Street. It was better known as 'The Coffee House.' It had belonged to the Newtown Coffee & Cocoa House Co. Ltd, a company set up by local businessmen in 1882. The company was wound up in 1907 and the business was taken over by the manageress, Mrs Francis. About 1920 the coffee house passed to John Pugh and his family.

Below: William Francis opened his ironmonger's in the middle of the nineteenth century. When he died in 1905 the business was carried on by his partners. It was taken over in 1924 by D.R. Davies, of Oswestry. The building was eventually demolished to make way for Boots the Chemist. The archway to the right remains, but the window of the North & South Wales Bank is now an entrance into Bear Lanes.

Left: The residential areas of the town were served by small general stores. These often took the form of corner shops like this well known one on the corner of Sheaf Street and Pool Road. It was run by Bessie Hudson, who is seen leaning on the stable door.

Below: Even further out of the town was this little shop on the end of Lilac Cottage, Nantoer.

The largest general stores in the town was the Co-op. It had outlying branches in surrounding villages. Branch No 1 was in Kerry.

This is branch No 2 being opened in Caersws.

Another rare indoor photograph of some of the staff of the Market Street headquarters of the Co-op. It was taken in the boot and shoe department. On the right is Jack Morris, the manager. The man in the light suit to the left is not a member of staff, but he certainly did wonderful things with a pair of boots. He is Stanley Matthews, the legendary footballer.

Instead of outlying branches, the smaller shops had deliveries by horse-drawn trap or motor van. 'Pop' Higgins had his bakery at No 37 Broad Street and here his daughter Rina does the rounds. Her husband Jack Pryce also drove the van, and until recently her son Malcolm carried on the family tradition as a baker.

The first motor delivery van in the town belonged to the Steam Laundry. It had a reputation for unreliability and its progress through the town was often frighteningly erratic.

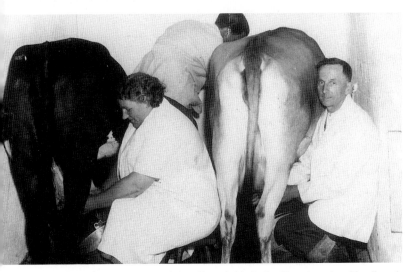

Before the days of fridges and freezers almost all perishable foodstuffs were produced locally and delivered daily. Here Mr and Mrs Harry Owen, of The Dingle, milk the cows in preparation for that day's round. In the background is Roy Edwards, who still has a milk business in the town.

It was a long time before motorised transport took over all deliveries. The railway horse-drawn drays and ponies and traps such as the one shown above were to be seen in the area until well into the 1950s. This picture from the 1920s was taken in Kerry, not far from the Co-op branch shown on page 81. On the right is Alonzo Lumsden (more usually known as Smith) who had a fish delivery business in the town. With him is his brother Jack, who became a police inspector in Manchester.

Seven

The River Severn

The river meanders along its old course past The Gravel in August 1968. On the right is the Rack Field, where woollen cloth used to be stretched and dried; on the left is the site of the town's gasworks.

The Severn has shaped the history of Newtown from its earliest beginnings. The first settlement was defended against attack from the north and east in the protective 'embrace' of the river. Later, the crossing at what is now the Long Bridge, gave access to the developing market town. In the nineteenth century the physical energy of the river was harnessed to drive the burgeoning woollen industry. It has never been possible for human agency to control that energy completely, and the catastrophic floods of the 1960s played a significant role in how the town developed thereafter. The river enters the town boundary at Dulas and at one time, a little way downstream, it met its first man-made obstacle – the weir that served the woollen mill at Milford. The mill burnt down in 1911, and afterwards the weir decayed and was eventually carried away by the waters. This picture shows it from the north bank of the river. On the far side there was a stone salmon leap, the remains of which can still be seen.

Until the estates at Trehafren and Vaynor were built the river flowed through open countryside to within a few hundred yards of the town centre. Sandy Bowers was a popular 'resort' for mothers with young children on summer afternoons.

The first bridge the river comes to is the Dolerw Park footbridge opened in 1973.

Before the town had its own swimming pool the length of river that ran between Dolerw and Newtown Hall Grounds served that purpose. Such customs were not without their problems. In 1911 four boys were fined a shilling each for indecent bathing near the tennis courts by The Cunnings. The fines were paid by their parents. One mother was heard to remark: 'Put them in the lock-up for an hour. It will do them good'.

This happy group of bathers was 'snapped' on Severn Green in 1937. Most of them still live in Newtown.

Looking upstream from the Long Bridge in the 1890s. Severn Green is on the left. At one time the stretches of river through town ran smoothly on account of the successive weirs serving the woollen mills.

The Long Bridge, from Severn Green, 1890s. This stretch of the river was once used for boating; the boats were launched from the Frankwell side, just beyond the arch of the bridge on the left. The little circular building on the right was in the garden behind the Public Rooms. The garden became a car park for the Regent Cinema in 1937.

The Long Bridge, so-called to distinguish it from the Short Bridge near The Gravel, was built to the designs of Montgomeryshire's first County Surveyor, Thomas Penson, c. 1827. It replaced an earlier wooden structure that crossed the river a few yards down stream. It soon became evident that it was too narrow to carry both vehicular and pedestrian traffic and there were a number of accidents, including a fatal one in 1853. The bridge was widened in 1857 by the addition of footways carried on cast-iron arches, again designed by Penson. Because of these additions the bridge is often referred to as 'The Iron Bridge.' The added footways, however, were never a great success. The surface of them consisted of cast iron plates which became very slippery in wet weather and many minor injuries occurred to pedestrians. There were also doubts about the structural stability of the ironwork. Additional ribs were added, under the direction of the then County Surveyor, Col Hutchins in 1906. After a long wrangle over who was to pay, the slippery surfaces were covered in Victoria stone slabs in 1924. In 1988 large wooden baulks were attached to the footways to prevent heavy lorries mounting the pavement to pass each other on the narrow carriageway. At the time of writing there is a proposal to make the bridge one-way. The problems of the Long Bridge remain.

Syars Mill and The Bridgend from across the river. These buildings were converted into the Catholic Church and Presbytery in 1947. Until the Over Severn Mill weir (a couple of hundred yards downstream) collapsed in the late 1920s, there was no fall in the river here, where the main sewer crosses from Penygloddfa. Dick the Boat's punts, seen tied up on the opposite bank made full use of this stretch of the Severn. This photograph is not all that it seems. It is a time exposure taken at night by moonlight.

The King's Bridge, rebuilt in 1930, was often called the Halfpenny Bridge and crossed the river from Severn Square to the Over Severn Mill. The two names are thought to have their origins in the fact that it was once a toll bridge. For many years the halfpenny tolls were collected by one Tommy King. An earlier wooden structure was carried away by the great flood of 1929. When it was opened there were immediate criticisms. Councillor Alfred Giles complained that it was too narrow, adding that 'there was not room for two fat men to pass'. He also claimed that it was not strong enough to withstand floods.

The river follows its old course downstream of the Halfpenny Bridge. The tall tree in the distance, in the centre of the picture, is a rare black poplar that at that time stood on the Llanllwchaiarn side of the river. It still stands, but is now by The Gravel car park on the Newtown side. It is the river, not the tree, that has moved.

The 1930 Halfpenny Bridge was removed when the river was widened and diverted as part of the flood prevention scheme. It was replaced by a post-tensioned concrete structure a few yards downstream. It is seen here under construction in April 1972. The concrete sections were laid on temporary trestles and pulled together by steel cables running through the bottom of each block.

The river used to meet the Bridge Wall by The Gravel. The culvert on the right is the outfall of the notorious Green Brook.

The Severn sweeps across what is now The Gravel car park and past the building that once housed Newtown Steam Laundry, now demolished. The shop on Pool Road, on the right, also demolished, was for many years a fish and chip shop.

The building of a second road crossing of the river had for many years been seen as a necessity. In 1902 it was suggested that such a bridge should be built to commemorate the accession to the throne of King Edward VII. The bridge, it was suggested at the time, would have the particular advantage of avoiding the need for funerals to go through the town to get to the cemetery. Work on this new bridge, however, did not begin until 1992.

The method of construction of the new bridge was similar to that of the Halfpenny Bridge.

Councillor Emlyn Kinsey Pugh, Chairman of Powys County Council, opens the new bridge on 8 April 1993. The Mayor of Newtown, Cllr. Jon Mackeen, is on the right.

Inspector Lyndon Clark, left and Sergeant David Crees escort the first cars across the bridge, 1993. The bridge, which leads from the site of the Cambrian Foundry to the site of the Cambrian Mill, was that day appropriately named Cambrian Bridge.

Green's Weir which provided water for the Craigfryn Mill, part of which remains behind Newtown Motor Garage on Pool Road.

NEWTOWN.
Pump House Weir.

Unlike the other weirs, the last one in the town – the Pump House Weir – was not used to drive a mill. Instead, it drove a water wheel to pump water out of the river to feed the canal. A simpler solution would have been to cut a leat from upstream of the Over Severn Weir from where the water would have flowed into the canal by gravity. But water was precious and the mill owners would not allow it.

The amount of water needed to fill the canal and feed the locks downstream can be judged from these two pictures. The Basin, now filled in and built over was the terminus of the Western branch of the Montgomeryshire Canal Navigation. The canal, which had been little used for many years, finally closed in 1936.

The waterway, after leaving the Basin, ran along behind Dysart Terrace, on the left of this picture. Although work is under way to re-open the canal it will only be possible, because of building and other work since the closure, to bring it as far as Aberbechan, just inside the town boundary.

'The Gro', Pool Road, on the Newtown side of the river, was once the vicarage occupied by the vicar of Llanllwchaiarn. The vicar, if he wished to avoid a lengthy detour, had to ford the river or use a primitive rope ferry. By 1887 Canon Evan-Jones had had enough of this and he organised the erection of a wooden footbridge. Because of its origin and ownership it became known as the Parson's Bridge. When Canon Evan-Jones died in 1925 he was not replaced, the rector of Newtown became also the vicar of Llanllwchaiarn. In view of this the canon's widow offered the bridge to the Urban District Council. They were not keen at first because of problems with the right of way to the south end and the state of the bridge. The UDC surveyor warned that 'there was a great risk of the structure collapsing'. By 1927 these problems were overcome, but two years later disaster struck. During the night of 12 November 1929 it was carried away by the worst flood in living memory. It is possible that its end was hastened by being hit by the remains of the Halfpenny Bridge which was also destroyed that night. The flimsy nature of the bridge is evident from the above photograph.

THE GRO BRIDGE, NEWTOWN.

The Urban District Council was reluctant to rebuild the bridge because of the right of way problems. Undeterred by this, the proprietor of The Bear Hotel, Ivo Smith, launched his own appeal for funds and entered into negotiations on the right of way. A committee was formed, and by April 1933 plans and funds were far enough advanced for the sod cutting ceremony to take place. The sods were to be cut on both sides of the river. There was a slight hitch when both ceremonial spades were delivered to the same side of the river, but Mr J.W. Ellis waded through the icy water and work began on both sides. The new bridge, now known as the Gro Bridge, was opened on 22 July 1933. Mrs Edward Powell of Plasybryn cut the ribbon on the Llanllwchaiarn side and crossed the bridge. She was greeted on the Newtown side by the Rose Queen of Newtown, Joan Stephens. C.W. Norton made a speech, Newtown Band played, the Pony Dancers danced and sports were held at the Gro Vicarage. The bridge was 'well and truly' opened. In 1946, however, the Gro Bridge went the way of its predecessor. It was carried away in a flood and was never replaced.

The unusual floods which carried away the Parson's and Gro bridges were by no means unprecedented. In 1852 a severe flood demolished the King's Bridge and almost every winter the river came into Severn Square and the streets surrounding it. But on the night of 3 December 1960 the town was struck by a deluge which seemed to exceed everything that had gone before. As well as filling its own course, the river tore through the streets of the town. It was not just the depth of the water that did the damage, but its speed. Debris ripped from one part of the town formed battering rams further down. No photographs exist of the peak of the flood that night, but this photograph of Broad Street taken at 8.50 the following morning gives some idea of the scale of the disaster.

The waters rush down Severn Place and on into Broad Street, December 1960. The large building on the left is the County Library at the rear of Plas yn Dre.

Debris floats into Short Bridge Street, December 1960.

Wally Davies, barber by trade and a member of Newtown Fire Brigade rescues a child in Gas Street, December 1960. The houses on the right, as far as the shop, remain. Those beyond, including the entrance to the gasworks, have been demolished.

Cecil Morgan's fruit shop in Broad Street was completely wrecked by the 1960 floods.

W.H. Hollinshead and Lloyd Barrett inspect the waters at the lower end of Ladywell Street, December 1960.

The rear of the Regent Cinema with the Armoury beyond, December 1960.

Above: The true course of the river became indistinguishable from the rest of the town. The large building is Shukers, agricultural engineers. It was originally built in 1937 as a garage, for no less than 225 cars, by John Cookson after his plans for The Checkers site had changed.

Left: The Halfpenny Bridge is in there somewhere. It survived, thus confounding the views that Councillor Giles had expressed thirty years before.

After the floodwaters had subsided experts said that a flood of this severity was unlikely to occur again for at least a hundred years. But experts are 'occasionally' wrong and almost exactly four years later, in December 1964, the river raced down Broad Street again.

Again in 1964 the water entered houses and business premises.

The Long Bridge once again was nearly submerged, 1964.

OLOGIES ARE OFFERED FOR THE INCONVENIENCE CAUSED BY THE DISASTROUS FLOODS OF LAST WEEK-END

WE RE-OPENED ON THURSDAY · AFTER ONLY THREE DAYS. COMPLETE NEW STOCK · PRICES KEENER THAN EVER

ORDER YOUR CHRISTMAS DINNER NOW – TURKEYS, GEESE, CHICKENS, PORK · ALL SUPERB QUALITY
VERY COMPETITIVE PRICES
ALL WEIGHTS AVAILABLE

The Spar Supermarket was wrecked for a second time.

Again the Halfpenny Bridge withstood a battering.

But Harry Harris, butcher of Commercial Street, managed to remain cheerful in the face of adversity.

Eight

The Life of the Town

Pictures of people at their place of work are hard to find, but here Les Syers, Bert Waring and Des Corfield put the finishing touches to Phillips' bicycles at the Lion Works in the 1950s.

This section looks at various aspects of life in the town over the years, starting with law and order. Until the 1930s Newtown was an Assize town. The Assize Courts, presided over by travelling circuit judges were held in the Public Hall (now the Regent Centre). At first the building was entirely suitable, but as over the years, it was converted first into a theatre and then a cinema it became more difficult to uphold the majesty of the law. At the 1936 Assizes, when the judge found a defendant not guilty as charged there was a loud outburst of applause. The judge said the outburst was most unseemly. He added that the building was 'more suitable for theatrical performance than for the administration of justice'. However, the judge's visits were not without a theatricality of their own. He would lodge overnight with a local worthy and in the morning be conveyed in solemn procession to the parish church where he would attend a special service before being taken to the Public Hall to conduct the business of the Court. In the above photograph taken in May 1912, Mr Justice Lush poses outside Crescent House, the home of the High Sheriff, local brewer W.H. Burton Swift, wearing the traditional knee britches and buckle shoes. On the extreme left is the distinguished local solicitor, Martin Woosnam. After the formalities there were five cases to be tried at the Summer Assizes.

The judge's procession makes its way along Milford Road and past Crescent House.

The judge's escort, a detachment of men from the Montgomeryshire Constabulary, poses outside the parish church. Note how the men in the front row have placed handkerchiefs beneath their right knees to avoid besmirching the blue serge.

The Scala Cinema became even less suitable for the administration of justice when it was enlarged and modernised in 1937. It was also renamed the Regent. George Black had become the manager of the Scala in 1924 and was retained by the new owners to run the Regent. He is seen here (wearing a bow tie) with his staff. At the front stands the doorman, Bill Morgan. The girls, from left to right: Ivy Williams, Marjorie Owen, Mrs Pugh Humphreys, Barbara Jones, Irene Francis and Chrissy Jones.

The cinemas and halls of the town were also used for occasional amateur productions. Newtown Amateur Operatic Society was formed in 1931 and this is a scene from their first production, *Maritana*, presented that year in the Victoria Hall.

Newtown Amateur Dramatic Society's November production of *The Holly and the Ivy*, 1955. The society was re-formed in 1935 although a group had existed in the 1890s.

This building, which once stood next to the Public Hall in Severn Place, was opened as The Montgomeryshire Infirmary on St David's Day 1868. By 1906 it was decided that a larger building was needed so a public appeal fund was opened. Land on Llanfair Road was given by Edward Powell of Plasybryn and the new County Infirmary was opened in 1911.

Almost immediately a progamme of extensions was begun, first a tuberculosis ward, then an outpatients department and in July 1929 the foundation stone of the maternity ward was laid by Mrs David Davies of Llandinam (above).

Mrs Edward Powell was a tireless worker for the welfare of the town. She is seen here with the local branch of the Red Cross at Plasybryn during the First World War.

For many years the children's clinic was held in the schoolroom beneath the Wesleyan Chapel. In August 1948 the mothers and babies were visited by T.R. Bridgewater, Chairman of the Food Control Committee, and Harry Pugh, Chairman of the Urban District Council.

Penygloddfa School is now the oldest school in the town. It was opened in 1847. The above part of the school, however, was demolished in 1987 to make way for new classrooms.

Ethel Bryers was a much loved teacher at Penygloddfa. She looked none to happy to be leaving when governors, staff and children gathered for her retirement presentation.

The foundation stone for Newtown Intermediate Schools was laid in September 1897 although the school had been in existence since 1894 in the Baptist Chapel. A boys' and a girls' schools were housed in the building and separation of the sexes was rigorously enforced.

A new block of classrooms was added to the school in 1937 and it was outside these that the headmaster, R.M. Kinsey was photographed with his staff on his retirement in 1939. From right to left, front: Mr Dean Jones (Chemistry), Miss N. Taylor (French), R.M. Kinsey, Mrs Kinsey, Mr W. Morgan (Latin), Back: Mr Beverstock (Maths), Mr E.G. Lewis (Geography and Mr Kinsey's successor as headmaster), Mr Hughes Jones (Welsh), Mr Harry Morris (Physics) Mr Eric Savage (Woodwork).

Newtown has always had a number of youth organisations. Newtown Scouts were formed in 1910. This picture is of the Rover Scouts *c.* 1930.

The 1st Newtown Company of the Boys Brigade flourished in the 1950s. Here they are at Sunday morning bible class in the Wesleyan schoolroom *c.* 1955.

Hockey has been played in Newtown for over a hundred years. The girls of Newtown County Intermediate School brandish their hockeysticks for the benefit of the photographer in 1903.

In 1940 the ladies of Newtown Hockey Club decided to take on the might of the British Army, there being a substantial military presence in the town during the war. This 'friendly' match was played on the Recreation Ground, formerly the RWW Sports ground. Any comment on the styles of play adopted by either side would be superfluous.

Newtown Golf Club, founded in 1895, had their first course on The Bryn Farm. It was not an ideal site, being very wet and exposed to the wind, so in 1908 they moved to their present site on Pool Road bringing their clubhouse with them. Members are seen above relaxing on the verandah soon after the move.

Tennis also has a long history in the town and for many years there were two clubs. These are the members of Hafren Lawn Tennis Club in the summer of 1935.

NEWTOWN F.C. - 1954~55.

W.MORRIS · G.WILLIAMS · D.L.JONES · G.JONES · R.MELLINGS · B.RIMMER · C.JONES

PHOTO: B.PASSANT.

WINNERS: MONTGOMERYSHIRE CUP · WELSH AMATEUR CUP · LEAGUE CUP

STANDING: E.RIGBY (PLAYER-COACH) [ROWLANDS (TRAINER) · G.LUMSDEN · J.EVANS · B.F.JONES · A.DAVIES · K.BOWEN · J.RICHARDS.

SEATED: I.OLIVER · D.POWELL · S.EVANS · E.P.WILLIAMS (CAPT.) · K.LEWIS · G.STEPHENS · P.THOMAS (ASST.TRAINER)

1955 was a momentous year for Newtown Football Club. They were triple champions, winning the Montgomeryshire, Welsh Amateur and League cups.

The scene is set at Latham Park for the Newtown *vs* Swansea final of the 1955 Amateur Cup. After the match the entrance in the foreground was named the Swansea Gate, a name it retains to this day.

It is not known whether Richard Humphreys was a sportsman in his younger days. If he was, it was a long time ago. It is nearly two hundred years since he was born in 1798. He lived to be 101, and had he survived a few more months he would have lived in three centuries.

Two more famous sons of Newtown. On the left is Mr Ll.C. Oliver, more usually known as 'Cammie' Oliver, a well known local barber and 'character.' On the right is George Hibbott who was awarded the MC in the First World War. He was an unarmed stretcher bearer with the 7th Royal Welch Fusiliers at the disastrous Suvla Bay landings in the Dardanelles. When asked why he had gone back up the beach under heavy enemy fire to collect another casualty, he replied: 'They were shooting at wounded men'.

In earlier pages Broad Street has been shown containing Newtown's most joyful occasions. This picture, however, shows Broad Street in what was, with hindsight, an appropriately sombre mood. When the First World War broke out, the 7th Volunteer Battalion of the Royal Welch Fusiliers was mobilised and billeted at its headquarters, Newtown. This picture, taken on 22 August 1914 is of the entire battalion of a thousand men leaving for Conway and from there eventually to the Dardanelles, Egypt and Palestine. Many of the men in this picture were never to return.

But before and after those grim events, pleasure-seeking crowds have gathered in the street. Here is a reminder of the heyday of the Royal Welsh Warehouse Sports Day.

More recently the old custom of gathering in Broad Street on New Year's Eve has been revived. This picture was taken just after midnight on New Year's Day, 1988.

It has been the intention in this book only to include pictures about which something is known. However, this one refused to be left out. All that is certain is that it was taken in the early years of this century and is of hundreds of children on the field below Hendidley, Milford Road.

And finally ... the picture that sums up the spirit of Newtown. The Green Brook frequently burst it banks in Dolfor Road, ran down New Road and into the houses in the Ladywell area. In June 1936 a series of severe thunderstorms led to some houses being flooded up to four times in a two day period. Elsie Tinker, Nora Thomas, Ivy Williams, Connie Williams and Megan Williams pause from mopping up in Bostock Place in the hope that the waters have finally receded. The cat on the roof is taking no chances. The location is easy to place as the windows at the rear of the Congregational Church in Park Street can be seen in the background. The ladies are standing in what is now Ladywell House car park.